AF072249

 Sound at Sight

Double Bass

Initial–Grade 8

by Tony Osborne

Published by:
Trinity College London
89 Albert Embankment
London SE1 7TP UK
T +44 (0)20 7820 6100
F +44 (0)20 7820 6161
E music@trinityguildhall.co.uk
www.trinityguildhall.co.uk

Copyright © 2009 Trinity College London
Unauthorised photocopying is illegal
No part of this publication may be copied or reproduced in any
form or by any means without the prior permission of the publisher.
Printed in England by Halstan & Co. Ltd, Amersham, Bucks.

Sound at Sight Double Bass Initial

• Initial

Only open strings with separate bows are used here.

Sound at Sight Double Bass Grade 1

• Grade 1

Use of first position is added and a dynamic change to notice.

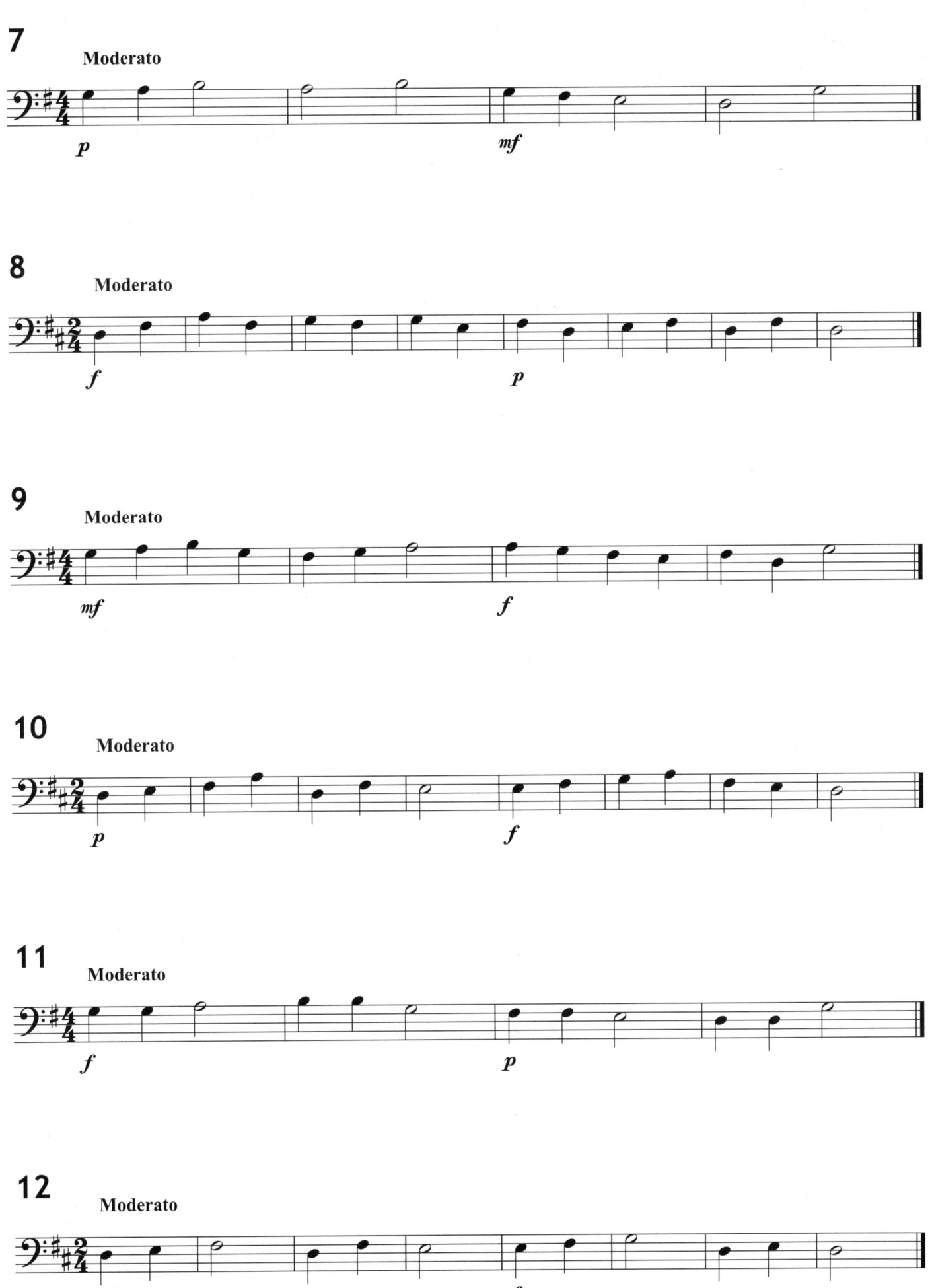

Sound at Sight Double Bass Grade 1

Sound at Sight Double Bass Grade 2

• Grade 2

Two-note slurs and ties are introduced.

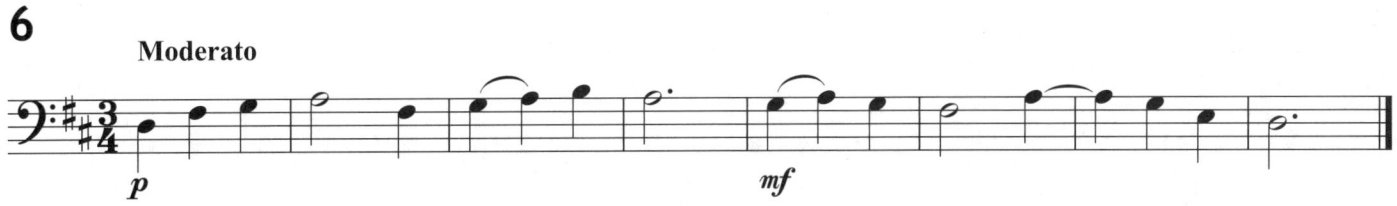

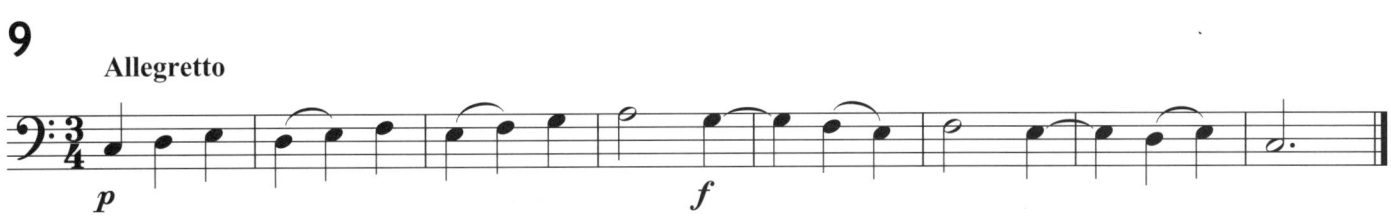

Sound at Sight Double Bass Grades 2–3

11
Allegretto

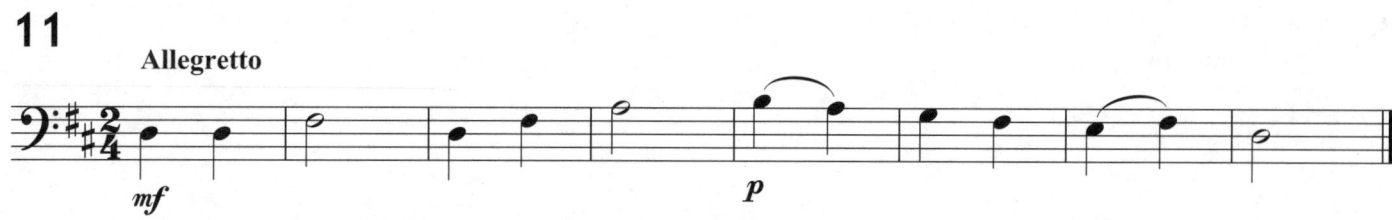

12
Moderato

● Grade 3

Half-position is added.

1
Moderato

2
Allegretto

3
Andante

Sound at Sight Double Bass Grade 3

Grade 4

Third position, changes of articulation and *pizzicato* are included in this grade.

Sound at Sight Double Bass Grade 4

Grade 5

Fourth position is new at this grade, as well as simple trills and harmonics.

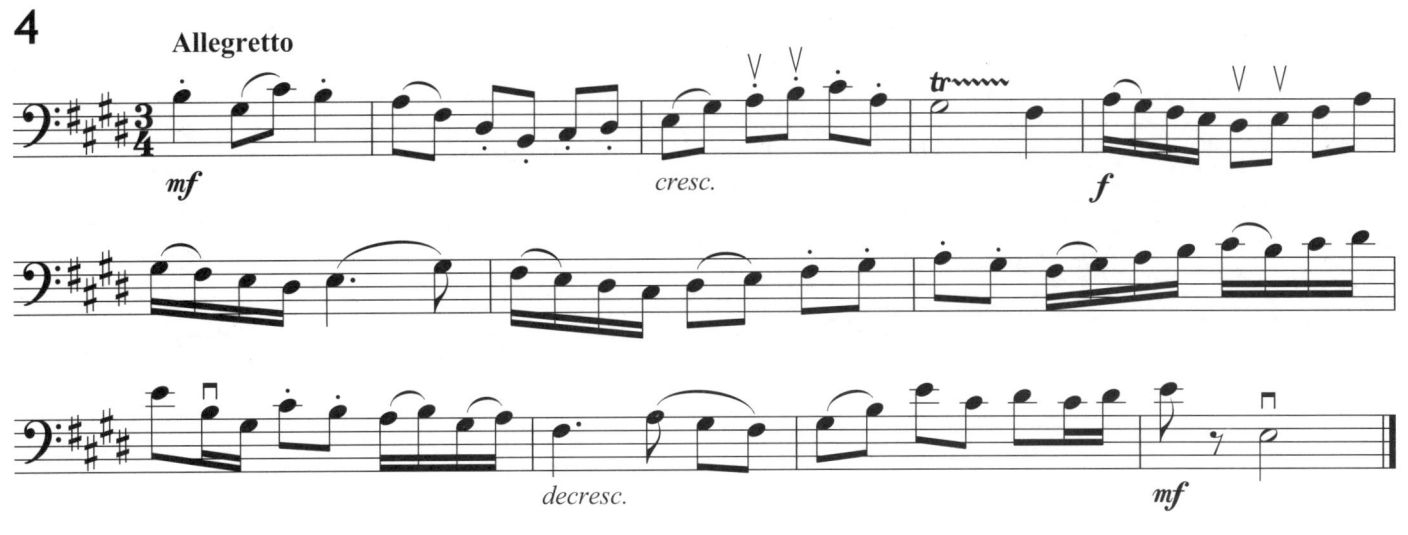

Sound at Sight Double Bass Grade 5

7

8

9

10

Moderato

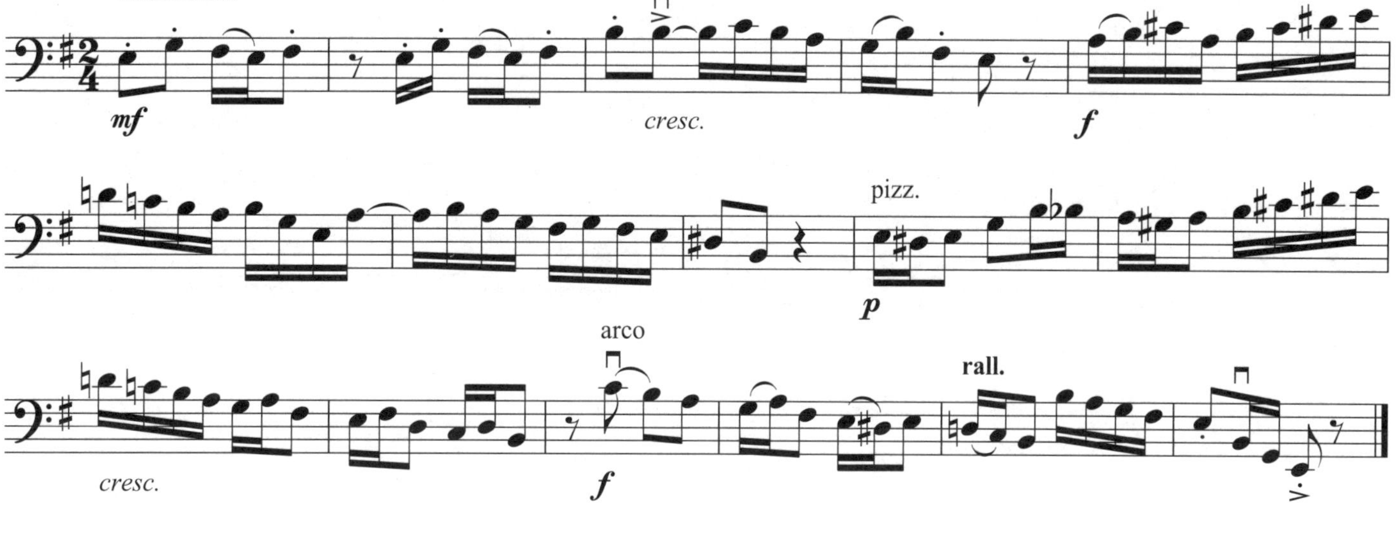

11

Moderato

12

Allegretto

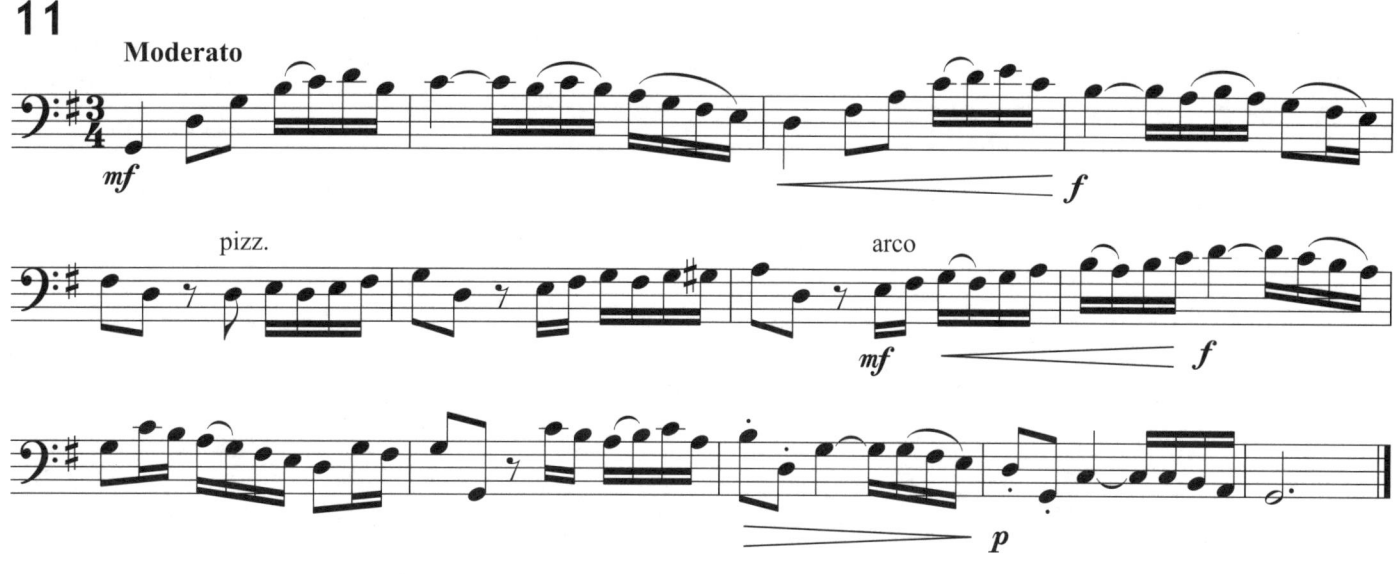

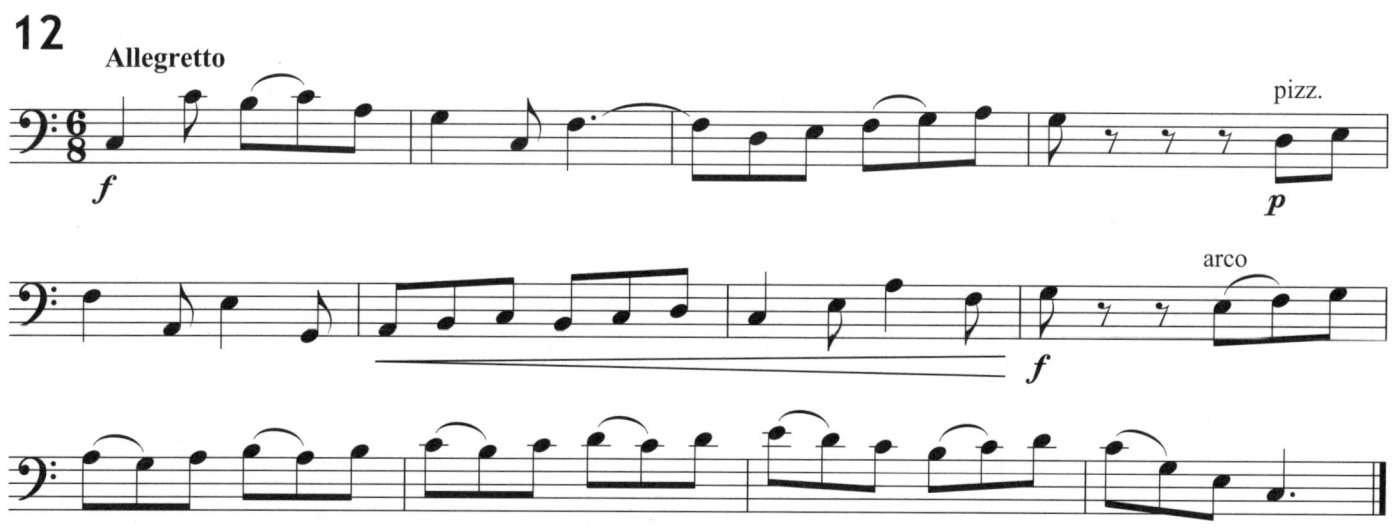

Grade 6

The left-hand notes have expanded up to fifth and sixth position, with use of two-note chords where one note is an open string.

1 Solid rock feel

2 Moderate gallop

Sound at Sight Double Bass Grade 6

6

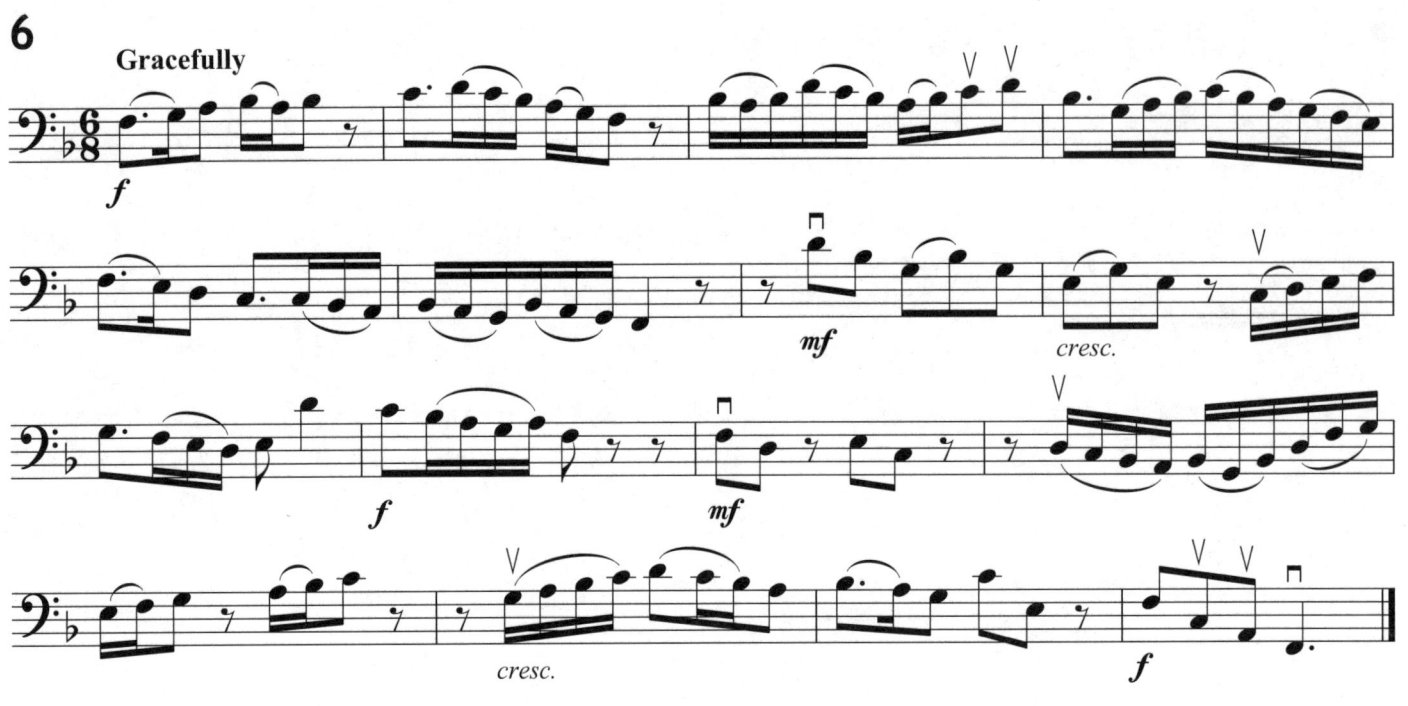

7

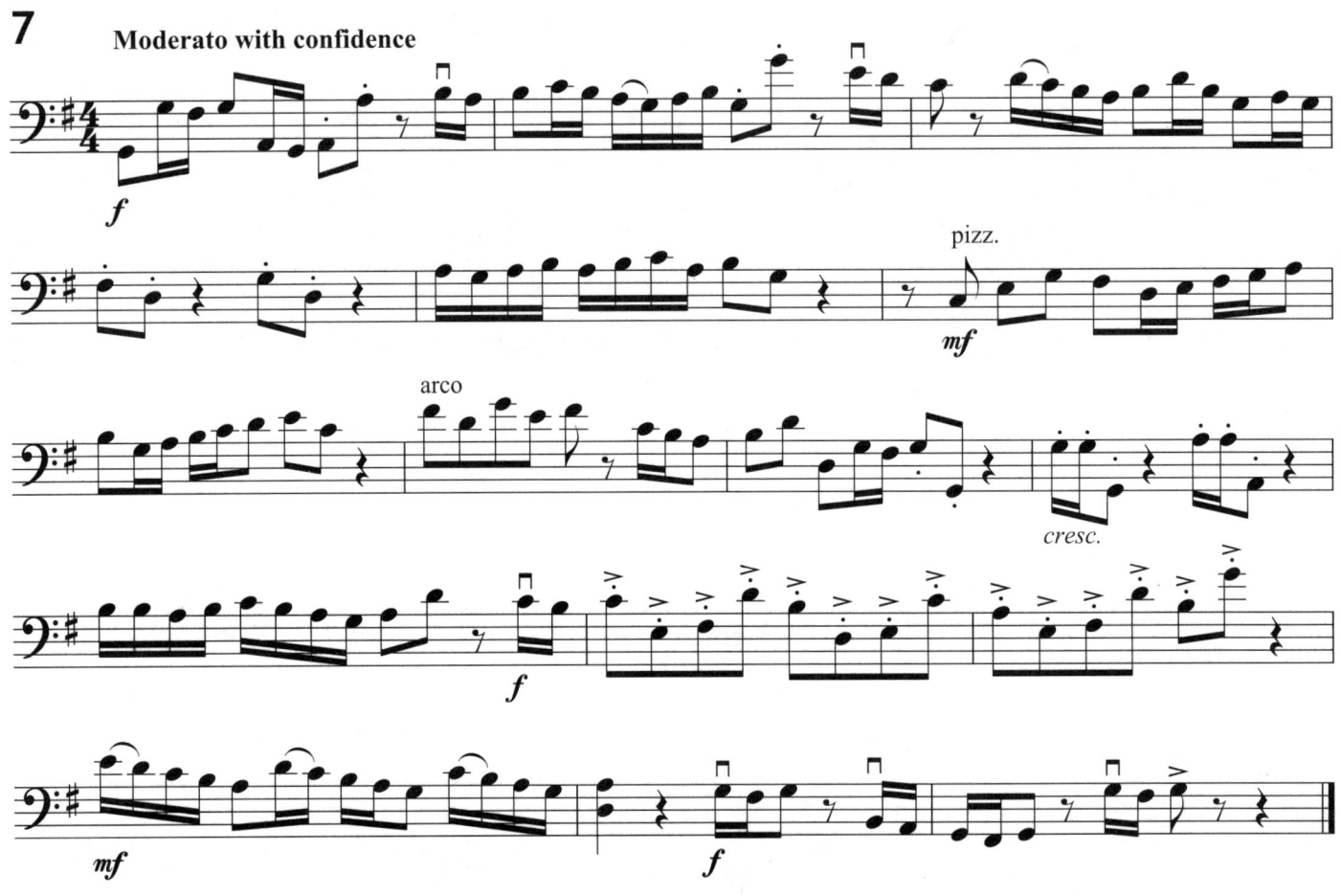

Sound at Sight Double Bass Grade 6

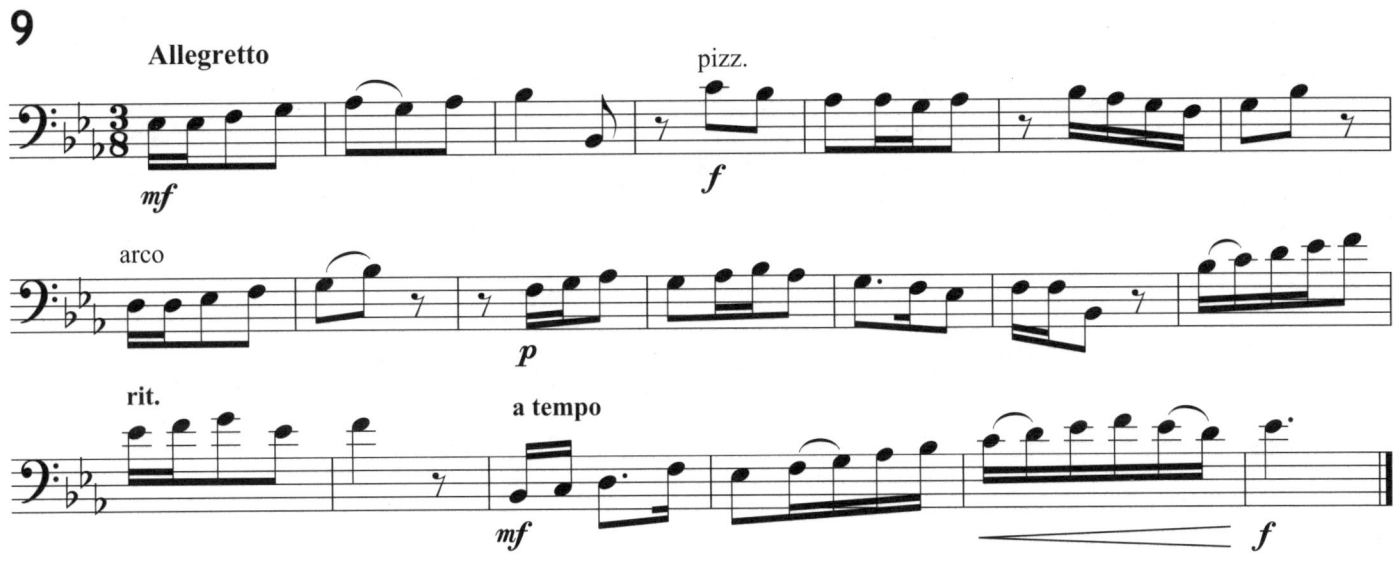

Sound at Sight Double Bass Grades 6-7

11 Moderato

12 Moderato in Latin style

• Grade 7

Thumb position implied by the treble clef and a closed hand shape is introduced, with new triplet rhythms and more frequent shifts and changes of articulation.

1 Flowing song

Sound at Sight Double Bass Grade 7

2 Blues style

3 Gently and smoothly

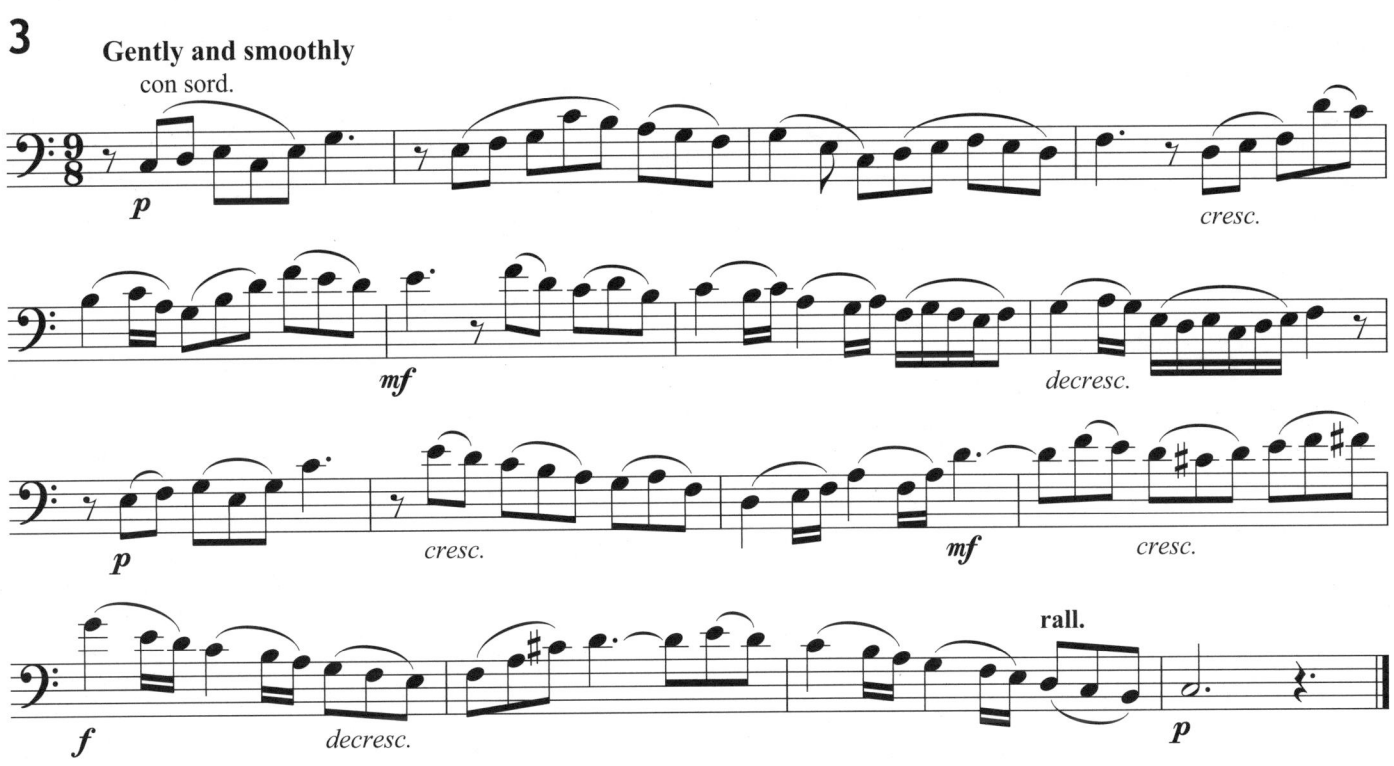

Sound at Sight Double Bass Grade 7

Grade 8

The tenor clef is introduced as well as time signature changes and duplets.

Sound at Sight Double Bass Grade 8

3

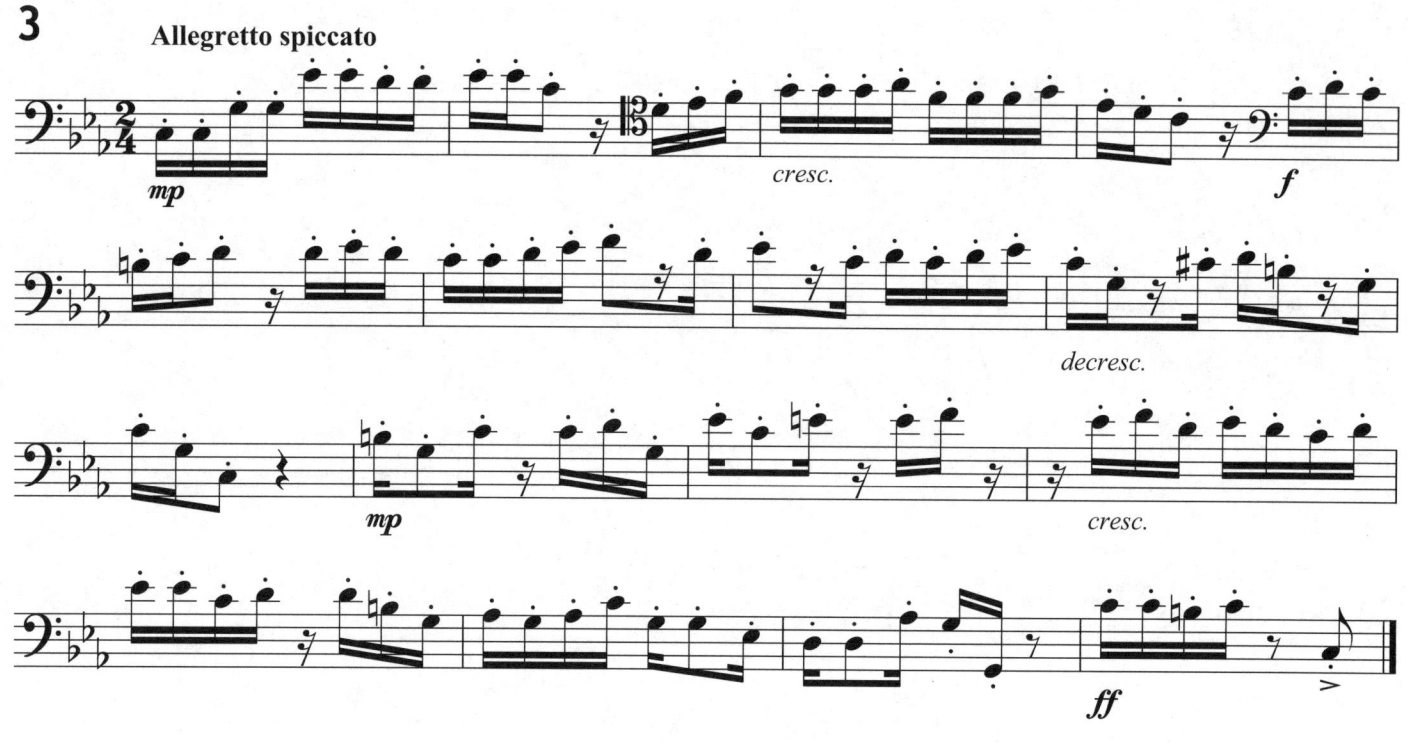

4

7

Gently flowing

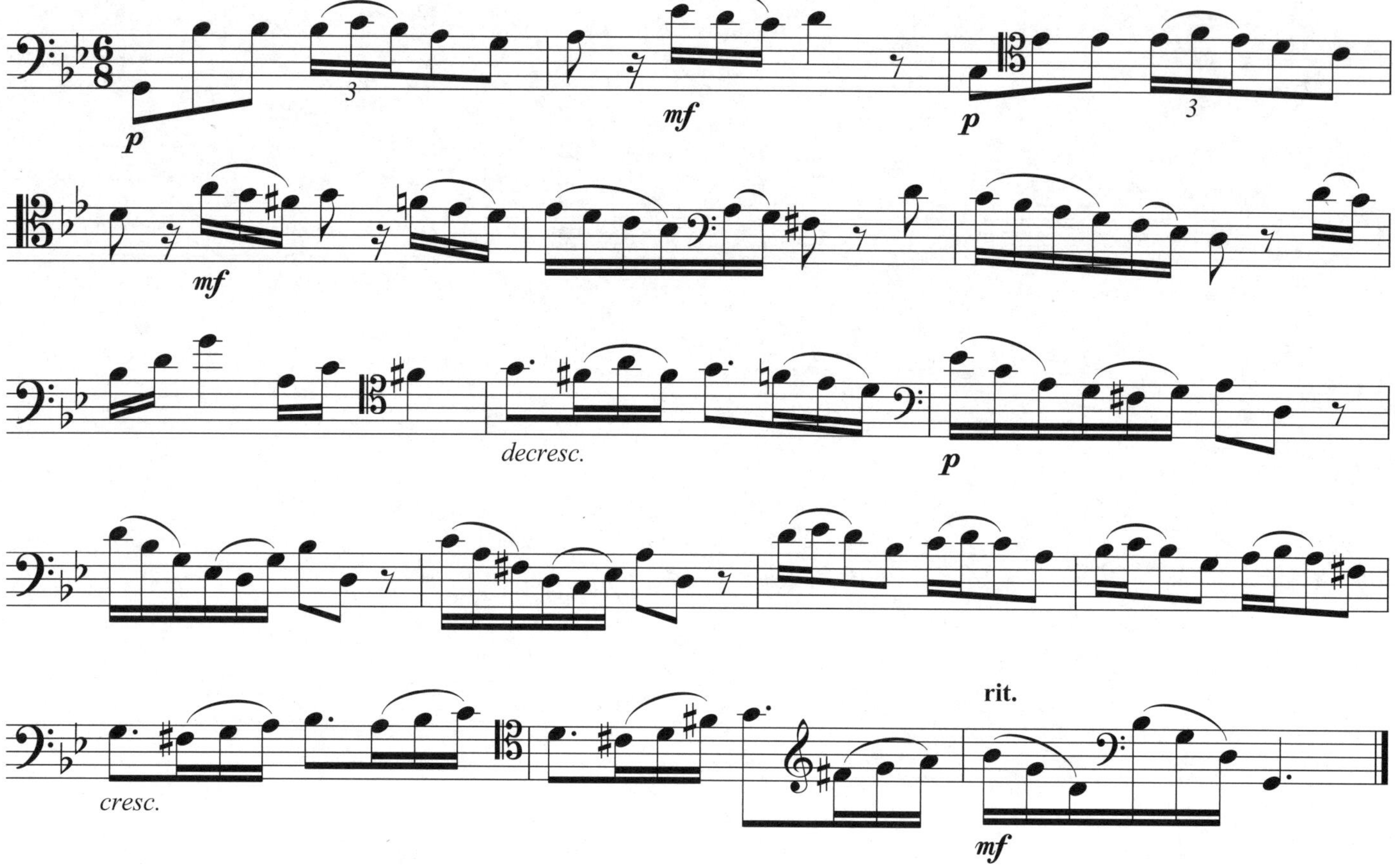

8

Steadily and boldly

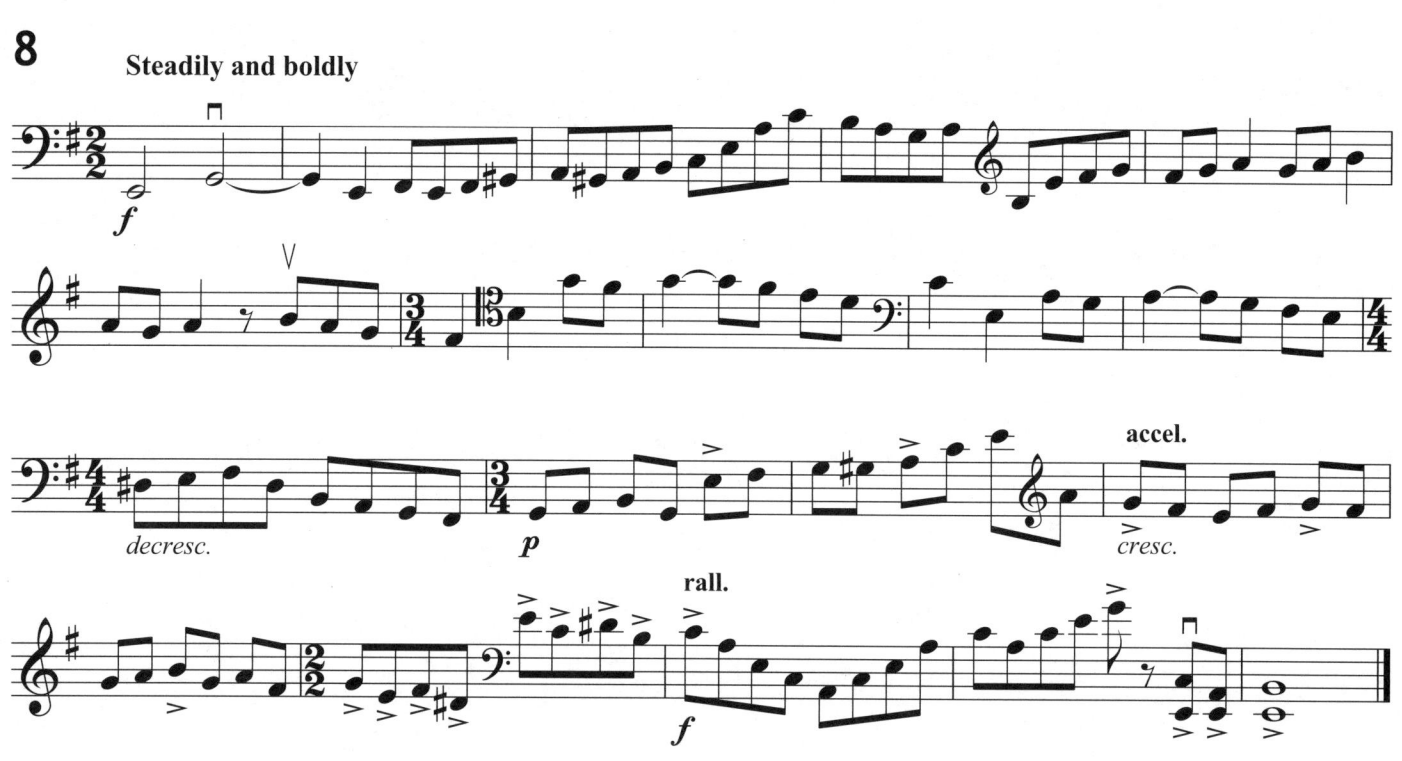

9

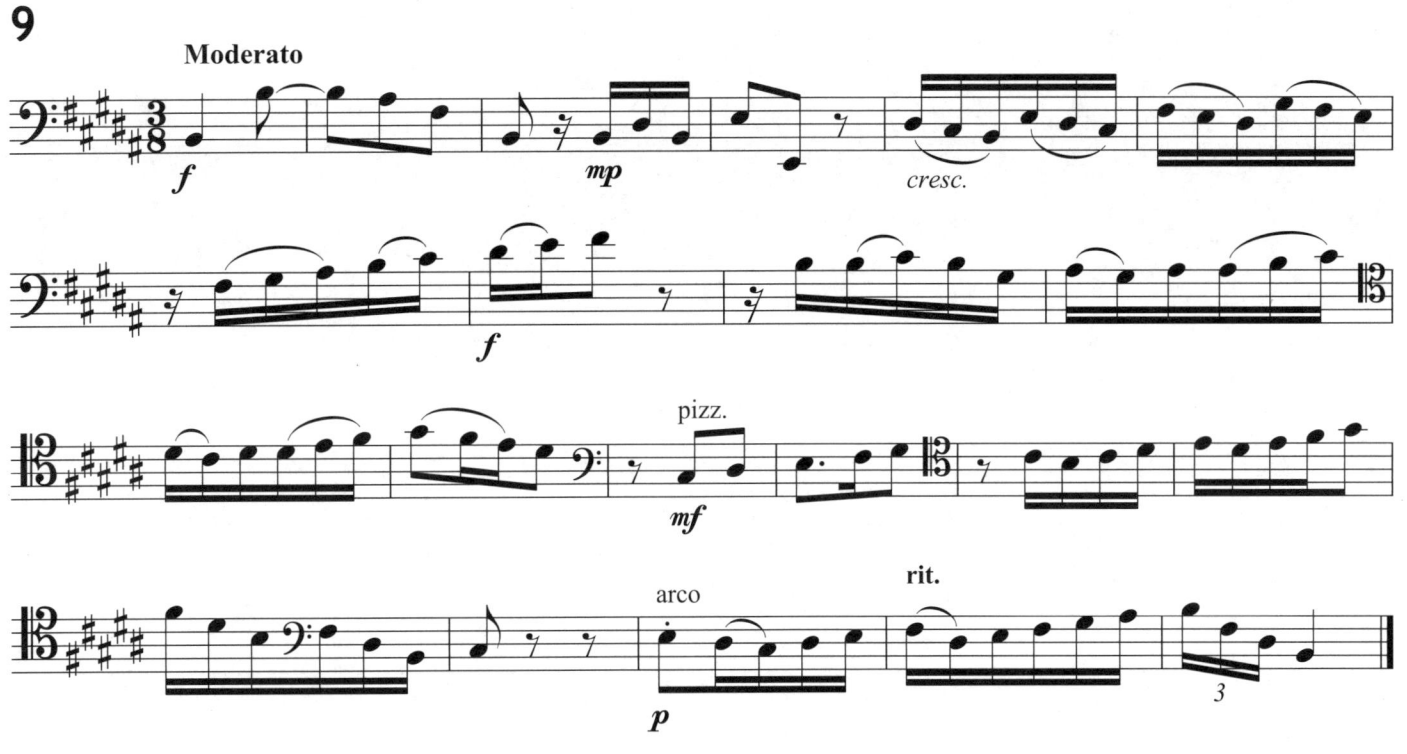

10

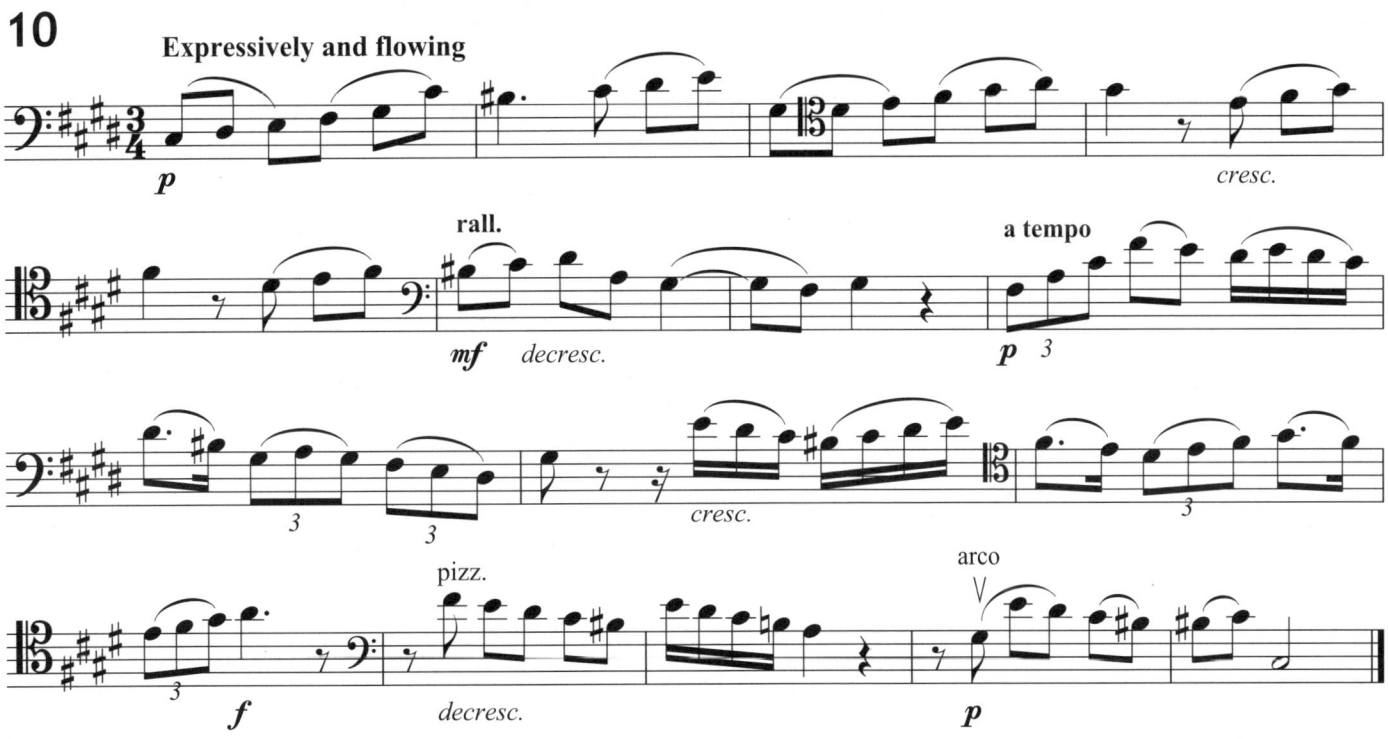

Sound at Sight Double Bass Grade 8

11 **Moderato in Blues style**

12 **Steady Latin American**

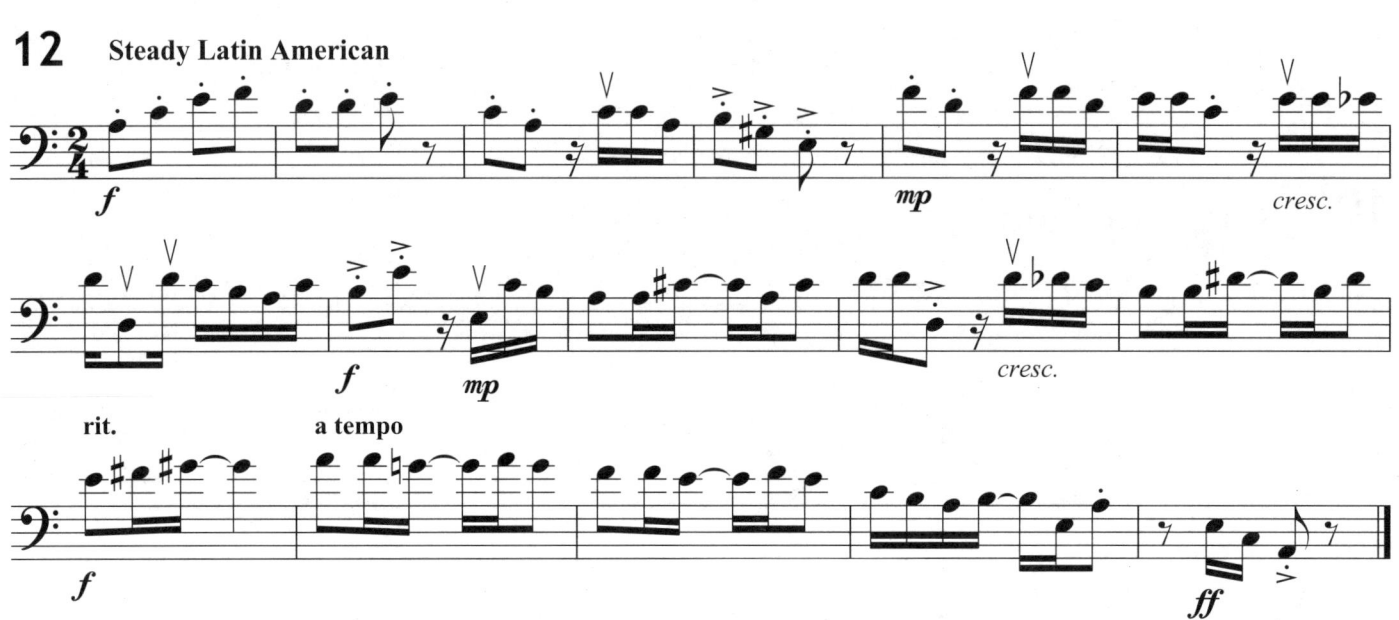